D0857438

The Smell of Matches

The Smell of Matches

John Stone

RUTGERS UNIVERSITY PRESS

New Brunswick   *New Jersey*

863442

Copyright © 1972 by Rutgers University, the State University of New Jersey
Library of Congress Catalog Card Number: 78-185389
ISBN: 0-8135-0726-X
Manufactured in the United States of America by
Quinn & Boden Company, Inc., Rahway, New Jersey

Since you have sown your brain seed in my brain,
I write for you thin poems
full of myself.
You say what they mean.

A poem is perhaps.

for my wife

Acknowledgments

Many people have helped in the preparation
of this book. I am especially grateful to:

Mae Nelson, who has typed and listened to me
and retyped and listened again,

and to Miller Williams, who knows what good
poems are and writes them, and who has
written Yes, No, or Maybe on early drafts
of many of the poems in this book.

Grateful acknowledgment is made to the following publications in which
these poems first appeared:

Beloit Poetry Journal: "An Example of How a Daily Temporary Madness
  Can Help a Man Get the Job Done"
Counter/Measures: "Bath and Bed."
Folio: "Coming Home"; "Tree"
The Lyric: "Medical Conference"; "Song for Tossing a Son."
The New Orleans Review: "Cadaver"; "Parts of Speech"; *"folie à deux:*
  one year."
Poem: "Lines While Waiting"; "Spider"; "It Is No Use"; "Bore"; "A
  Morning of Wind."
Poetry Northwest: "In the Bath."
The Random House Anthology of Contemporary American Poetry:
  "Living With a Voodoo Doll"; "Linda"; "To a Fourteen-Year-Old Girl
  in Labor and Delivery"; "Cadaver."
Raven (University of Alaska):
  Vol. 1, No. 1: "Piano Lessons"; "Changing the Glasses"; "Gardening
  Editor Dies In His Garden"; "Love Poem for a Son"; "For Two Sons
  Sleeping"; "Getting to Sleep in New Jersey"; "The Crossword Puzzle
  Maker."

Vol. 1, No. 2: "Donkey House"; "The Ophthalmologist Buys a Candy Bar in the Concession For the Blind"; "Holding Our Breath at Bedtime"; "Poem Said by My Son on Learning that His Toy Soldier Has Lost an Arm."

Shenandoah: "The Bottle."

Southern Humanities Review: "Changing Places"; "Stroke"; "An Old Icebox"; "Lines for a Last Class."

Southern Poetry Review: "Resuscitation"; "To a Fourteen-Year-Old Girl In Labor and Delivery."

Sumac: "Dali"; "Amnesia."

Western Humanities Review: "A Note for Theodore Roethke."

Contents

An Inch of Water

for my mother

A Note for Theodore Roethke

I will tell you what I know.
Sleep is quick, waking slow.
Words will work if said just so.
Even the smallest flowers grow
and one by one the children know
what is now is now has been.
The eyes open but shut again.

Cadaver

"The initial lesion of syphilis may result over the years in a gradual weakening and dilatation (aneurysm) of the aorta. This aneurysm may ultimately rupture and lead to death of the patient." — medical textbook.

Fitting the labels
in our books
to our own tense tendons
slipping in their sheaths

we memorized the body
and the word

stripped the toughened skin
from the stringing nerve
the giving muscle.

Ribs sprang like gates.

In the chest
like archaeologists
we found it:
clotted, swollen,
aneurysmal
sign of an old sin—

the silent lust
that had buried itself
in the years

growing
in the hollow of his chest

still rounded by her arms
clinging
belly to belly
years beyond that first seed

to the rigid final fact

of a body.

To a Fourteen-Year-Old Girl
in Labor and Delivery

I cannot say it to you, Mother, Child.
Nowhere now is there a trace of the guile
that brought you here. Near the end of exile

I hold you prisoner, jailer, in my cage —
with no easy remedy for your rage
against him and the child. Your coming of age

is a time of first things: a slipping of latches;
of parallels like fire and the smell of matches.
The salmon swims upstream. The egg hatches.

Lines on a Misread Word

> ... "bones and muscles" in his
> science book having been misread
> as "bones and musicals" by my
> seven-year-old son.

My own bones are tired of talk;
they make no music when I walk,
but our skeletons together
have brought us nearer song than either
could have come to on his own.

And he will sing yet—not alone,
but, with some lighter female struts,
he'll dance in the air above these streets:
the two of them loop in the sun like kites
and not come down for days or nights

but sway like notes from xylophones
that play inside their musical bones.

Lines While Waiting

What do you care

that in the blue dusk
his arm cracked
like a tree branch

the green bones sprung
like the tines of a fork
and the tears running
silver lines

into the wells
of his astonished ears.

Two Dreams of Leukemia

Where will he spend tonight
Mr. Claridge
who gave my secretary perfume
that once he sold for $50
before he was weak and his marrow
had turned against him.

And the other nights
what of them
of the women he used to see
and give Nuit d'Amour?

He will stretch out again
in the Chevron station
taken in by the evening crew
to the smell of oil and gasoline
the thump all night of Coke machines
to wait the predictions' coming true.

While he dreams
of what he was and would have done,
of whatever he had wanted to keep,

Elaine lies in her own sleep,
her arms crossed like a nun's,
the perfume he gave her
blooming on her wrists like flowers.

Holding Our Breath at Bedtime

Against the clock we hold our breath
and for a minute mimic death

except our lungs puff out our cheeks.
We each look for signs of leaks

or laughs or cheating. The one who wins
is he who grimly shuts off grins

and flutters of the diaphragm.
This game reminds me that I am

thirty years of breaths ahead.
Your seven-year-old face is red

with trying what I've tried before:
to put off sleep a minute more,

play dead and hope it passes by.
The clock moves on; and, with a cry,

you gasp, pant—and I have won.
I tuck in your stretch and yawn.

That is the part I want to save.
Air is what we *have to* crave—

air and water, food and sleep.
But love is why my breath was deep:

this breath was one I'd wish to keep.

Stroke

I imagine his bedroom
where he woke this morning
to find half his singing nerves
numb and silent

his tongue halved and pulling
the cold words cramping in his throat

half a world gone in each eye.

I dream
his darkened bedroom
where last night
his mind meshed
in its last unaltered thinking

where now
these work shoes
will unwalk
neatly
against the wall.

Bath and Bed

If one can drown in an inch of water,
this is enough for fifteen girls.
What does this careful cleanness matter,
except for the baby. And why the curls

except for the businessmen one meets.
(The towel is rough against my breasts.)
I choose a gown of soft blue lace.
It has been two years since my face
burned the razorless night on these sheets.

Who will see through my negligee
or watch the scales for my hint of fatness?
Even the reading light is gray.
His half of the bed is perfect flatness.

Explaining About the Dachshund

There's no badger in this sandbox.
There wasn't one here when I nailed it
four feet square and hauled
the sand ten miles.

There's not one in it now
despite this nosing
nosing around these tunnels
we dug by hand.

It's genes that have caught up with him,

an instinct for fur some ancestor
had to leave behind,
tremble-jawed but safe,
in other ground.

It's a grandfather's failure

makes him want to kill
something he hasn't seen
but can't forget

that comes back with him now to the house,
part of his cells, and sleeps beside him
in the red-eyed dark of my kitchen,

mixed in with the other smells.

A Morning of Wind

The wind is hot before rain.
Elbows propped in my window
I watch boys toss news of yesterday
to empty porches.

The welded weeks clank together.
I have shed my daily skin
in the wind of ten thousand mornings
like this one.
My stubbly beard is always growing.

Slowly I learned
    the winds are inconstant
the stars are deadly glass strewn
    on the sky
    the sun forever
        cancers the eye.

Now
I am an old man undershirted

and flesh is incurable.

Medical Conference

During the past year two children have been lost in London
following accidental ingestion of large amounts of digitalis.

> Lost in London: green leaves float
> among the red cells and a coat
> of fox-glove stops the heart and throat.
>
> The children lie now, slack of vein,
> lost in London, where they have lain
> for one full year.
>
> "It is plain
> the drug may act to slow conduction
> through the node with the production
> of A-V block."
>
> The long instruction
> grinds, ends in the usual way.
> All I have heard the speaker say
> is they were lost in London.

The Crossword Puzzle Maker

When the letters refuse
to fit into place,
she thumbs her dictionary
for words she's never used:
ancient Egyptian gods
and planets, Emperors
and gnus.

Over my morning coffee
I am unaware of her,
the blocks and blur
of her hop-scotch mind.

Nor can she know,
who holds back answers
for tomorrow's paper,

what my world is about,

the corners
I have worked myself into,
with no words to get me out.

Talking to the Family

My white coat waits in the corner
like a father.
I will wear it to meet the sister
in her white shoes and organza dress
in the live of winter,

the milkless husband
holding the baby.

I will tell them.

They will put it together
and take it apart.
Their voices will buzz.
The cut ends of their nerves
will curl.

I will take off the coat,
drive home,
and replace the light bulb in the hall.

An Old Icebox

There was a click
when the door closed
and the light
went out of his brain

with only the air
he brought in with him
plus that which he later
hunted in the corners

together with the smell
of old meat and vegetables

and the one-way joke
he had played on himself

back of the door
to outside

and Charlie and Jim
going home for supper.

All he could see
was what he could hear

the factory whistle
trains rumbling

blood tumbling
in his ears
for half a day
before they found him

God!   Alive!

dazed, dry
as a wilting flower

liable, innocent
in the same hour.

Resuscitation

When the heart coughed
and the lungs folded
like flowers
your eyes had barely closed.

By all signs and proper science
you were dead

warm and dying
in one unmerciful
and unelectric instant.

Sweat hung
in my eyebrows
like a father's.

It is easier now
to reconstruct
your death in life.

Now four days later
as you play at trains

I can remember
when the blood began
to bump like boxcars
in the back of your eyes.

finis

All that needed saying has been said.
The world implodes in silence in its shell.
The tree grows dying and the seed is fed.

The fall is filling out the year in red
while water freezes in the open well.
All that needed saying has been said.

The leaves drop spinning from a spider thread.
The spider stops its spinning in a spell.
The tree grows dying and the seed is fed.

The plunging horses know what lies ahead;
the spokes are turning faster than the wheel.
All that needed saying has been said.

We set the hands and we began to dread
the grinning clock-face and the private hell.
The tree grows dying and the seed is fed.

The heart learns truth more slowly than the head,
yet in your eyes I knew and I could tell
all that needed saying has been said.
The tree grows dying and the seed is fed.

The Bottle

Summers ago, after the woman
had moaned and birthed it
onto little more
than a kitchen table,

he sealed it in a bottle
while the sun bore down
and the patients waited.

In that long bath
it remains a monster
that couldn't live in air
but lasts in formalin

its forehead pressed against
the glass as though
against an endless window.

What magic did he use it for?
What lesson did it teach him

or his patient,
frightened anyway of what
the doctor might have to say
over his glasses

and the fetus
twenty years old on the shelf
staring at them both

believable as any genie.

The Five-Toed Sloth

and for my sons,
prodigal,
and perfect
in every imperfection
love is.

In the Bath

I believe what you are

as you rise over
the two-kneed camel,

the whale's belly,

and the five-toed sloth
drowns without a struggle.

Treacherous, you lap
my nose like an island.
Deeper, there is
a double roar:
the sea in the shell,
the red cells looping
in the brine my mother made.

We are all swimmers,
inside and out.

Water and salt
sustain us till
the spit of the last trumpet.

The sound you make
leaving
is the suck of animals
down a vortex

a sound learned
in the long canal.

Now one-thousandth
of my daily skin
is gone, grown, gone again.

I will leave a ring
where we last met.

Love Poem for a Son

I begin with you,
not red and wailing,
but small and round
in the upper tube,
where X met Y and multiplied,
in the soft cave of the uterus
where you caught and hung;
when notochord was spinal cord
and gut was gut forever;
when eyes were large,
as they still are;
and the heart was gathering
blood like flowers;
and what you started with
had to do.

You curled and uncurled
before the first breath
of anything but fluid,
and the thump of the mother
heart gave motion and all magic,
till you moved out like a little boat,
and came to me, red and weeping,
as even now you sometimes do.
I end with you.

Changing Dogs

To keep a growl inside the house,
to put off death in a world of stuff,
they kept substituting Spitzes
in a succession of bark and howl.

Any whitish dog was enough:
male or female, son or mother —
none of that could make much matter.
Sex was a ball of fur we never
understood too well anyway.

How many different dogs there were,
I was never sure. It was all one
dog to me and to my brother.
In a parade of paws they came,
white-haired, black-eyed, smelling
the same, panting and jumping into all
our joy and whatever sadness there was.

                    I think now
of the nights we must have slept
much better for not knowing how
they leaped at trucks and cars or when
they ended. Of how we were rarely sad,
although several times bereft of this love
that said goodbye but never left.

Being There

A doctor yourself,
    and you, a doctor's wife—
I like to believe
all you would have needed

was a kitchen table,
an aerosol of carbolic acid
against the bacteria seeding
from the cellar,
towels and water,

a teething ring
(from the first child)
for you to bite together.

Still I wanted you to know
how with a sweat, a smile,
an anxious cough,
my arms around you both,
I delivered your baby
from a long way off.

for Sandy and Jay Smith

Parts of Speech

1

Some of these words
are ten years old.
They have rolled
about in my brain
and wrinkled
to end up here on this
definite
paper.

2

Instead of words
what would you have me use:

motions?

signs?

breathing?

while the crazed heart see-saws
in its bony cradle
at every word
you
never
say.

3

hic   haec   hoc
huius   huius   huius

and the word declines.

Getting to Sleep in New Jersey

Not twenty miles from where I work,
William Williams wrote after dark,

after the last baby was caught,
knowing that what he really ought

to do was sleep. Rutherford slept,
while all night William Williams kept

scratching at his prescription pad,
dissecting the good lines from the bad.

He tested the general question whether
feet or butt or head-first ever

determines as well the length of labor
of a poem. His work is over:

bones and guts and red wheelbarrows;
the loneliness and all the errors

a heart can make the other end
of a stethoscope. Outside, the wind

corners the house with a long crow.
Silently, his contagious snow

covers the banks of the Passaic River,
where he walked once, full of fever,

tracking his solitary way
back to his office and the white day,

a peculiar kind of bright-eyed bird,
hungry for morning and the perfect word.

For Two Sons Sleeping

Early morning. I tell time
by the size of the shoes
I stumble over in the dark

and they are larger
by my measure
since last week.

O great growing toes!
Between bursts of
basketball and small cars,
between the start and finish
and the final basket,

O feet,
keep still a minute
and let me think.

How wake them gently
to what I do,
home late
from the lup-dup
of sick hearts

or tell them
that what I do,
what we all do,
dies

how talk to them
without answers,

them snaggle-toothed,
stirring from sleep
to play,
growing their feet,
growing new teeth
before I come back tonight.

The Ophthalmologist Buys a Candy Bar
in the Concession for the Blind

Punching up the day's accounts
in her black and holy Braille,
she totals up exact amounts
with a stainless silver nail.

At times she dreams some customer
will nudge her with a knife or gun:
her hands will hand the money over,
her blinded throat will find the phone.

But, mostly, children come like elves
in the noise of this canteen
to pick the cabinets and shelves
of candy she has never seen —

this mistress of the try-and-fail,
blind beyond my knife or lenses,
who from the sameness of her jail
sees past all my other senses.

Afterward, He Watches the Ceiling

This is the way we pay the human coin:
cheek to humane cheek, loin to loin.

You the banker, I the smiling wreck,
we turn and countersign the personal check.

And, dollar down toward final willing cent,
I, who can still afford you, am well spent.

Going Back: The High School Band Room

There is no sound.
Basses bloom
on the last row.

But now in a practice room, a trumpet
goes up comes back goes up
in half-steps.

And people are drifting in.

Waldo has come back
round as the tone of his clarinet
his best tune *Deep Purple*
in the lowest register
back from his last ditch
and his wrecked car.
He fakes the faster passages
like a master.

Another is putting together
the long bones of his bassoon;
a girl the fingers of her flute.

Where the drums march,
Don is tapping the snares,
tightening them like Krupa.

Howard rips his trombone.

The baton rises, drops,
and we have put down our cruelty

for this one hour,
a long way from the tambourines
and wood blocks we started on.

He is back.
We are playing.
He is back. His long hair is slick
and does not move with his arms.
We are playing together.
The sound surrounds us like heat.
He has taught our separate heartbeats,
teaches us time for all time.

Song for Tossing a Son

Bag of flour, sack of sand,
I toss you up and watch you lean
in air twice distant as my hand,
and higher than my head has seen.

The cry you make is one part terror;
the other half is laughing boy.
You fly with all my human error;
I bring you down with careful joy.

When you are older, wise and sure,
may you regain this oval track
that lets you rise in thinner air
till love and gravity pull you back.

Donkey House

There was no donkey
for the tall grass that crept
around it like snakes.

For months it was
a checkpoint for the bands
of bandits that roamed
the creek and canebrake.

But it was only a stable

three sides against the wind
and a wooden trough
that used to glow like a fireplace
with corn and hay.

As soon as the match was set
the stable raged

tongues leaping
smoke rising like ghosts
the word roaring like fire
through the neighborhood.

It was not until morning
when the fullness of the burning
was realized
and the dogs were sniffing
the ashes

that we thought
perhaps something holy
had lived there.

Amnesia

Three days black: the day of the fall
and one on either side. The crack
in your skull is leaching lime

to put back into place all
the mind that leaped out like a pack
of frenzied dogs. For you the time

since that misstep on the ledge
is a mirror that follows you back and back,
but leaves you at the edge.

for D. N.

A Thirty-Four-Year-Old Substitutes as Goalie in Little League Soccer Practice

They are running
but I am out of breath.
My tie blows like a pennant,
green and yellow striped reminder
of what I must be tomorrow.

But now I am goalie.
The English in my blood
kicks at my ribs
watching the play.
My son, seven, at the end
of the field, runs
on his shin guards as though
he were born to them.

And they are coming my way,
miniature stallions,
snorting, faces contorting
toward the goal.

Boot it! Boot it!

and the boy boots it
with the energy of all
his eight years,
like a cannon ball,
but into my hands

and I have it,
I have it.

My toe dents the ball
to yells of victory.

And I trot to the sidelines
to huddle tall with my teammates
and my son,
sweaty, tired, proud as a bruise.

Coming Home

About two thousand miles
into my life
the family bounced south
west   east
in an old Oldsmobile.

Two brothers tumbled
on the back seat
watching the world blur
upside down right side up
through windows
time fogged in
slowly from the corners.

Nights
cars came at us
wall-eyed
their lights sliding
over the ceiling
like night fighters

while in the front
they talked parental   low
in a drone
we didn't hear ·
tossing through Arkansas
toward Mississippi.

When our eyes grew red
and blood bulged
in our heads from laughing
we slept

he on the seat
and I bent over
the humped transmission

close to the only motor
in the world.

Linda

Seven, frog-legged among the boys,
even now you realize
what magic holds mechanical toys

have on them. In the green sway
of a sun-burst tree you compromise
the zoom and sputter of their play.

Then you rise, shake off the grass:
you are seventeen, and wise;
their long necks bobble as you pass.

Their gaudy noise halts and garbles.
You know their automatic eyes
are rolling after you like marbles.

Changing the Glasses

Ten and curly, you came
suddenly one morning
like measles.

Since then I have watched you
small, large through lenses

seen your acne come and go,
the braces on your teeth
necessary as a smile.

God! You have been beautiful
growing to match your eyes.

I have been a pair
of bald bifocals,
blurring beside the lines
of letters.

I have settled for your eyes,
once a year,
pupils wide as midnight.

Today, twenty,
you came for contacts,
blinked while I fit them
to you like precious stones.

After you left
I wished you

strong-eyed children

everything
in focus

even the edges perfect
as the first crystal
of a crystal.

Tree

I was used to you
and your countable
branches.

What is this sudden
bursting into leaves?

Lines for a Last Class

It's just as well: it was no use going farther.
What I have given I gave like a father
and you took like a son

which means that many of you will remember my face
but nothing I've said. For whatever use
I leave my blessings, too.

I have taught Atlanta rather than Xanadu.
(Build your own palaces.) Would you
have known the difference?

Nothing I have said could have been deleted.
Be careful, though, what is repeated
outside the walls of this room.

New students are waiting to be seated.
Class is over. You may go.

Gardening Editor Dies in His Garden

He depended on the seasons,
knew the damndest things:
the best pH for fescue;
the reason concrete underground
yellows the leaves;
metabolism of thrip and mite.

Tonight the trees blow and blow
and crickets click like
his typewriter which, somehow,
never got rid of all the crabgrass.
He staked his life
on no late frost, on no disease
without a treatment, on recipes
against tomato blight.

A hundred thousand readers
fell forward with him
in his garden.

Now, two weeks after,
his last words cling
on the page like ivy.
Dallis grass blooms high
as lilies while aphids suck
the undersides of leaves.

And who is to warn us of winter?

da capo

So many mornings

in the long fraternity
of the house,
my cheeks puffed with sleep

till you,
your face rough with lather,

woke me conducting Brahms
and Bach by record

with your razor.

Rehearsal took ten years.

When I saw you last
you conducted an orchestra
we would have dreamed of
had we known enough.

Stravinsky stirred and laughed.
Mozart was still unburied.

Afterward
sprawling in a chair
you told me again
about music.

Grace notes poured
out of you like sweat.

for Samuel Jones

Playing Ball with a Left-handed Son

Your world spins incorrectly, son.
I watch you throw and kick and run:
all your English is reverse.

Sinister doors should turn about,
since going in is coming out.
Even the classroom has a curse:

your fingers move and drag your wrist;
the ink smears; your letters list.
Now you watch while I rehearse

the longer pass, the dextrous goal;
you mirror it to gain control
and teach yourself the true converse.

What you do now, I did worse.
When I am clumsy, you will be deft;
for what is left is right, my son,
and what is right is left.

One Eye Blurs

Living with a Voodoo Doll

Hair and nose and eyes like mine,
I made you, doll, to look like me
from teak and paper, bits of twine.
I place you in your chair for tea

to tell you what my world is like.
About the phases of the moon,
the way a pin becomes a spike,
how I have danced and to what tune.

All evil signs I leave for you:
red threads of worry for your eyes,
the sleeplessness and deep tattoo
of wrinkles, the pain. You realize

that yours is mine to take or give.
And I could kill you.
                            I make you live.

folie à deux: one year

(*folie à deux:* psychosis occurring simultaneously in two associated persons)

The sound of trucks
is closer than the wheels.

Can you know how deeply
you have sown your brain seed.

How shall I say
the world worried you.

Why are we where
are we how are we bound.

Should I let you know the bones
of my brain are slowly crumbling.

Shall I tell you that your little
madness is like these raindrops
dimpling the puddle of my mind.

The right eye blurs; the left
sees much too clearly—I keep
them both.

Can you also hear the long trucks
rifling toward morning on this
same dumb air.

Beef Tongue

Knuckles of pigs
in the next compartment
rap on the glass, but you
cannot hear, separate as you are
from your ears.
And a new shipment
of brains has come in,
unelectric, but perfect.

Tongue,
foot-long, stiff, cold
with cellophane,

tongue
that lately larruped your calf,
rolled alfalfa down,
and licked the salt,   '

there are enough parts in this store
for some new animal

a myth that might somehow
work with a brain,
beat with a heart,
pump incredible insulin
from these sweetbreads,
bile from the liver,

and bounce from the store
on strong filets and hooves.

If I could bring you back together,
tongue,
I would,

rather than have some human,
less well hung-together,
crisscross his knife and fork
in the fat and gristle
of your final moo.

60

Spider

I found him
deep in moonlight
weaving a spell around my house.

It took three squirts
to kill him
at the center of his universe
to fill him
with poison till the unspun web
clotted in his fingers.

Early this morning
on my way out
he was still dead.

Beyond, the streetlight
gleamed like a moon
against his world
where he shriveled
at the center
like a rubber band.

Bore

Your mouth yawns red
like a fresh river trout.

When you are dead
maybe that mouth

will hang open
and every important word

you never said
will drop out.

After Supper

my brother waits for me
in the dark throat of the house,
poised like a beast
under the bed
behind a chair
by the long white teeth
of the piano.

I hope to spot him
as shoes beneath the drapes
an extra shadow

but he has had time enough
to find a place
where his eyes will not glow

his lungs can be quiet

his grin not show
until he pounces.

It is better to
have it over with

let him leap out
with a cackle
spring arms
at my shirt

and let my dreams
digest him
while I sleep.

A Little Sequence in Which
I Become a Maestro

My hair will have to be longer
my nostrils instructed to flare.

I will ask the violins
to play F against F sharp
until it sounds natural.
Sweat will oval
under my arms.

There will be hands
clapping inside my ears
as I step off the podium

and come down the stairs
like tympani.

Piano Lessons

She wanted me to stretch my fingers
into next week   and next week.
I mean stretch them,
pull the tendons in their joints,
loosen bone from bone a bit.
My hands were too small
for octaves,
too little for recitals,
Chopin and Brahms,
which she would have had me
playing even now
except I escaped
by moving to a larger town.
Here she will never think
to look for me.
My fingers can be normal.
And I can disguise myself
as a clarinet,
march past her in the crowd
lining the street for parades
and blow her eardrums out
with a high held G.

Digging

My son is following
a tree root to its source,
learning connections,
dirt and purpose
all at once.

He has attacked it before,
but from topside,
monkeying the limbs.

He shows me the branches
underground,
makes me believe
there are leaves on them
in some different season

when we must come back and look.

66

The Crane

In the sandbox
overnight
while the boy slept
and dreamed

his toy crane grew,
became a giant of steel
squatting by the house.

At the first word
boys came, savage
with pleasure,
on legs flashing
in the sun like scissors.

Windows went first,
all the collected reflections
that looked out and in.

In a maze of gears
a workman aimed
the wrecking ball
and brought down in a day
what took years
to call home.

The foundations lie now
like a fortress.
Steps go up and down.
In the broad new sunlight
of the cellar
ants crawl in the cracks.

Outside the Cave

Knee, hand, Neanderthal,
I squat on Sunday afternoon
and wrench up dandelions one
by one. Beneath my feet, the long roots crawl,

turnip-tender; leaves both green and pallid:
I watch with prehistoric eyes
this pile of dandelions rise
that once I might have tossed for salad.

An Example of How a Daily Temporary
Madness Can Help a Man Get the Job Done

My brother knows the man
who really is Smokey the Bear.
I have seen a picture of him
wearing his other head
and smiling his human teeth
into the camera.

Days
he feels, walks, sweats,
and talks to campers.

Nights
he lives in Memphis
under the name of Simpson,
sleeping off the woods
and the smell of fire.

Mornings
he puts on the fur suit,
and goes to work
only a little madder
than the day before.

It is the stares he draws
driving
that keep him going.
The hairy head
slips over his,
and the darkness closes
around him, deep
and comfortable
as a growl.

Changing Places

Today I will be the blind man.
I will turn off the lights,
bump into walls,
and feel the blood
leak out under my skin.
I will be drunk with blackness,
uncertain as one foot
before the other.

Then I will put my feet
on the desk and look.
The light will break over me.

Tonight the stars will burst
like flares.
Tomorrow I will be deaf.

Poems Said by My Son

1

On Learning that His
Toy Soldier Has Lost an Arm

We're made of wood.
Our heads won't come off.
We won't come apart. See?
We can say yes.
We can say no.

2

Once upon a Time

This used to be a turtle
but somebody stepped on it
and it changed into a rock.

It Is No Use

We have surrounded your house.
We number thousands
and we will saw through the walls
if necessary to reach the tunnels
of your ears.

It is understandable
you thought the noise
was a dog scratching at tree roots

the screen door uneasy
on its hinges

water coughing in the pipes.

We will know if you whisper fear
out of the side of your mouth
as you stare
and pretend
we are only crickets.

Dali

Since I was six
and didn't care

girls have been
exploding in the air
around me like figs.

One burst
yesterday in that chair
became
a bearded man in minutes.

Only three I know
who haven't blown up:

One found her voice
gravelled overnight.

Another plucked
hair from her nose —
ovaries dangled from the end
like fruit.

The last one
is puffing up,
showing signs.

It is a matter of time.

Every year breasts drop
to the ground
like apples.

What the Hormones Say
a study in jazz

They say
yes
to the sixteen-year-old girl
all wobbly pelvis
belly sway
and yes
to her baby in a blind
nose dive.
Yes to breasts and yes
to milk
and maybe
to the father
in molecules.

Yes to the sprouting
bathing boys
yes to pickles
and all that tickles
in their groins.

And maybe
to the young man,
one more time, say hey,
say hey,
just one more time.

And what do the hormones say
old man?
Say no,
no

in a hundred things.
No
in a choir of benzene rings
and double bonds,

in the wedding ring
now grown to the bone.
No,
old man, alone,
alone.

Autopsy in the Form of an Elegy

In the chest
in the heart
was the vessel

was the pulse
was the art
was the love

was the clot
small and slow
and the scar
that could not know

the rest of you
was very nearly perfect.

KNEEDEEP: A Kind of Love Poem

The Biogenetic Principle: An individual member of any species repeats roughly the early stages of development of all other species.

I watch you, tadpole, super-sperm,
on the way to frog from worm
while you feel your form unfold or
shrink your tail or shape a shoulder.

What I thought was mouth instead
begins to blink within your head.

Find your legs somewhere inside
and the throat that tries to hide
above the roundness of your belly
buried knee-deep in this jelly

of weeds, algae, snails and mud.
I would not change you if I could.

This is my birth you re-create,
swimming proof that each must wait
for what the other has to be.

I celebrate the you in me.

for many people

ABOUT THE AUTHOR

John Stone is a physician in Atlanta, Georgia. He was born in Jackson, Mississippi, in 1936, and received his B.A. degree from Millsaps College. He graduated from Washington University School of Medicine (St. Louis) in 1962, and later trained at The University of Rochester Medical Center. He is married and the father of two sons. He is Assistant Professor of Medicine and Assistant Dean at Emory University School of Medicine and Medical Director of Outpatient Services at Grady Memorial Hospital.

The text of this book was set in Melior Linofilm and printed by Offset on P & S Special Book manufactured by P. H. Glatfelter Co., Spring Grove, Pa. Composed, printed and bound by Quinn & Boden Company, Inc., Rahway, N.J.